FooFoo's Ballet Dream

Dedicated to Noor and Emir

FooFoo's Ballet Dream Dedication:

Dedicated to Noor and Emir

By Waleed Hamada

Waleed Hamada, loving uncle.

Once upon a time, in a meadow tucked between the woods and the mountains, there lived a curious little rabbit named FooFoo. She wasn't like the other rabbits, who loved hopping, digging, and nibbling on carrots all day. FooFoo had a dream, a dream to become a graceful ballerina.

One sunny morning, FooFoo tied ribbons around her paws to look like ballet slippers. She twirled and leaped across the meadow. Her friends; Squeaky the squirrel, Tilly the turtle, and Benny the bird watched with wide eyes.

"You're so graceful!" chirped Benny.

"But rabbits don't do ballet," said Tilly. "We're too bouncy!"

FooFoo just smiled. "I'll practice and prove we can."

That morning, FooFoo sat in the meadow, carefully tying ribbons around her paws. Each ribbon was bright and colorful, just like her dream. As she finished, she looked at her reflection in a little puddle and smiled.

Nearby, her friends couldn't help but stop and stare.

"She's really doing it!" squeaked Squeaky the squirrel.

Benny flapped his wings. "I think she'll be amazing!"

As the sun dipped lower in the sky, painting the meadow in shades of gold and pink, FooFoo began her ballet practice. She twirled, leaped, and stretched her paws as gracefully as she could. Her ribbons danced with her in the breeze.

"You're flying, FooFoo!" cheered Benny.

"Such high jumps!" exclaimed Squeaky, clapping his tiny paws.

Even Tilly, the slowest and calmest of the group, gave a slow and steady cheer. "You're getting better, FooFoo."

FooFoo smiled. "I'll practice every day until I'm ready for a real stage!"

One bright morning, FooFoo found herself standing in front of a grand outdoor stage nestled between the trees. The stage was adorned with colorful flowers, glowing softly in the sunlight. It looked magical.

FooFoo held her ribbons tightly, her heart fluttering like Benny's wings. "What if I trip? What if I forget my steps?"

"You've got this!" squeaked Squeaky.

"We believe in you!" added Tilly and Benny in unison.

FooFoo took a deep breath, gazing at the stage. This was her moment to shine.

As the sun set and twinkling fairy lights illuminated the stage, FooFoo stepped into the spotlight. She spun, leaped, and twirled with grace, her pink ribbons fluttering like butterfly wings.

The audience, a crowd of forest animals watched in awe. Benny flapped his wings excitedly, Squeaky clapped with all his might, and even Tilly looked thrilled as she cheered loudly.

FooFoo felt her nerves melt away. This was her dream coming to life. With each movement, she danced not just for herself but for everyone who believed in her.

As the final notes of her performance faded, FooFoo bowed deeply, her heart swelling with joy. The meadow erupted in cheers and applause. Benny, Squeaky, and Tilly rushed to the stage with a small bouquet of wildflowers.

"You were amazing, FooFoo!" exclaimed Benny.

"We always knew you could do it!" said Tilly.

FooFoo smiled, holding the bouquet close. She gazed out at the crowd of forest animals, all clapping and cheering for her. At that moment, FooFoo realized her dream had come true, not just because she danced, but because she had shared her joy with everyone.

From that day on, FooFoo became the meadow's first ballerina, inspiring animals near and far to follow their dreams, no matter how big or small.

FooFoo's Ballet Dream Dedication:

Dedicated to Noor and Emir

Waleed is a man whose love for family drives
him to excel and live every moment to its fullest!
We as a family that have been taught that giving
back is the greatest gift that one could give,
and this book gives my niece and
nephew a piece of history.

Written By Waleed

www.ingramcontent.com/pod-product-compliance
Lightning Source LLC
Chambersburg PA
CBHW080128150626

46550CB00017B/2831